SPACE EXPLORERS

ARTIFICIAL SATELLITES

by Jenny Fretland VanVoorst

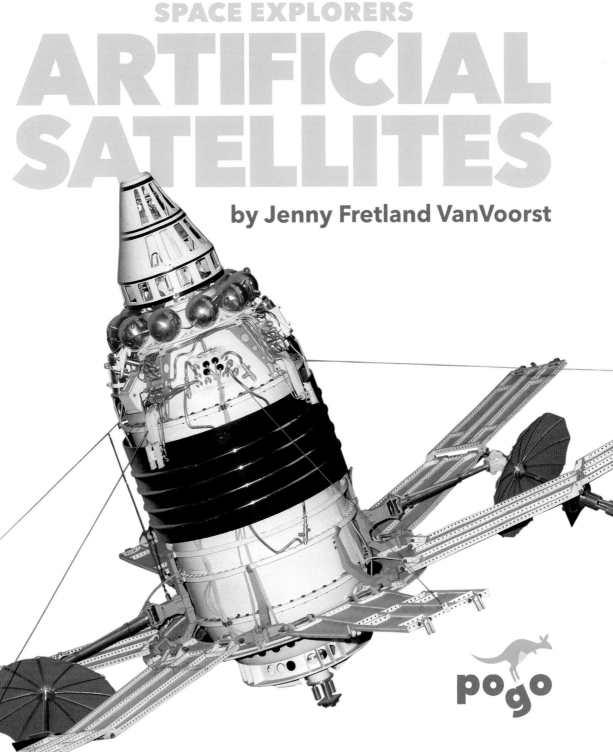

pogo

Ideas for Parents and Teachers

Pogo Books let children practice reading informational text while introducing them to nonfiction features such as headings, labels, sidebars, maps, and diagrams, as well as a table of contents, glossary, and index.

Carefully leveled text with a strong photo match offers early fluent readers the support they need to succeed.

Before Reading

- "Walk" through the book and point out the various nonfiction features. Ask the student what purpose each feature serves.
- Look at the glossary together. Read and discuss the words.

Read the Book

- Have the child read the book independently.
- Invite him or her to list questions that arise from reading.

After Reading

- Discuss the child's questions. Talk about how he or she might find answers to those questions.
- Prompt the child to think more. Ask: Have you ever seen a satellite pass overhead at night?

Pogo Books are published by Jump!
5357 Penn Avenue South
Minneapolis, MN 55419
www.jumplibrary.com

Library of Congress Cataloging-in-Publication Data

Names: Fretland VanVoorst, Jenny, 1972- author.
Title: Artificial satellites / by Jenny Fretland VanVoorst.
Description: Minneapolis, MN: Jump! [2016]
2017 Series: Space explorers | Audience: Ages 7-10.
Includes bibliographical reference and index.
Identifiers: LCCN 2016014029 (print)
LCCN 2016014450 (ebook)
ISBN 9781620314128 (hardcover: alk. paper)
ISBN 9781624964596 (ebook)
Subjects: LCSH: Artificial satellites–Juvenile literature.
Scientific satellites–Juvenile literature.
Outer space–Exploration–Juvenile literature.
Classification: LCC TL796.3 .F74 2016 (print)
LCC TL796.3 (ebook) | DDC 629.46–dc23
LC record available at http://lccn.loc.gov/2016014029

Editor: Kirsten Chang
Book Designer: Molly Ballanger
Photo Researcher: Kirsten Chang

Photo Credits: All photos by Shutterstock except:
Age Fotostock, 20-21; Alamy, 12-13, 18-19; debra millet/Shutterstock.com, 3; Getty, 15; Science Photo Library, 11; Science Source, 4, 8-9; Thinkstock, 16-17.

Printed in the United States of America at Corporate Graphics in North Mankato, Minnesota.

TABLE OF CONTENTS

CHAPTER 1

UP IN THE SKY

Look up! What's that light in the sky?

It's not a star. It's a satellite.

A satellite is an object that circles another body in space.

Some satellites are natural. The planets in our solar system are satellites. They **orbit** the sun.

Earth has one natural satellite—the moon.

It also has more than 1,300 **active** artificial satellites. Why?

natural
satellite
(moon)

artificial
satellite
(International
Space Station)

Earth

satellite
image

We use them to look at Earth, the stars, and other planets. We use them to study the weather. Some help us communicate. Others are used for **spying**.

DID YOU KNOW?

The first artificial satellite was *Sputnik I*. The Soviet Union launched it in 1957. It spent 92 days in orbit. Then it burned up in Earth's **atmosphere.**

CHAPTER 2

WHAT'S ON BOARD?

Satellites serve many purposes. But they all have a few things in common.

solar
panels

All have a power source,
such as **solar panels**.
They also have a battery
to store the power.

All satellites have **instruments** that keep them in contact with Earth. They can take pictures. They can send messages. They also receive instructions and path changes from **ground control**.

DID YOU KNOW?

Some satellites stay in space after they've stopped working. They orbit Earth as "space junk."

CHAPTER 3

EYES IN THE SKY

Satellites are eyes in the sky. Countries use them to gather information on their enemies.

In 2003, the United States went to war with **Iraq** based partly on evidence from spy satellites.

Satellites are used for science, too. Some look down at Earth. They help scientists predict storms. They show how the earth changes over time.

DID YOU KNOW?

Satellites don't just orbit Earth. Mercury, Venus, Mars, Jupiter, and Saturn have all had scientific satellites orbiting them.

Other satellites look outward.
Space **telescopes** look far into
the solar system and beyond.
They send back photos that
help us understand our universe.

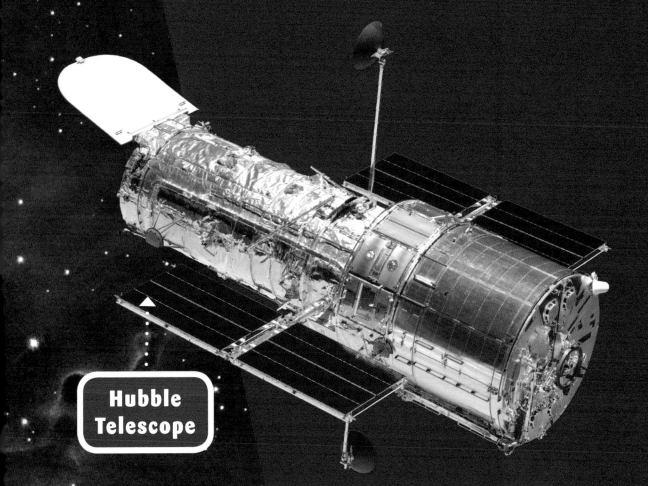

Hubble
Telescope

Communications satellites help people on Earth connect. They make cell phones possible.

Artificial satellites are our eyes—and ears—in the sky!

TAKE A LOOK!

How do communications satellites work?

1. You make a call. Your cell phone sends a signal to a tower.

2. The tower sends the signal into space. It is picked up by a communications satellite.

3. The satellite sends the signal to a tower back on Earth near where your call is going.

4. Finally, the second tower sends the signal to the phone of the person you're calling.

ACTIVITIES & TOOLS

TRY THIS!

BE A SATELLITE SPOTTER!

More than 100 satellites are large enough to be seen with the naked eye. Do you think you can spot one?

1. Go outside at dawn or dusk.

2. Look up into the sky. Keep your eyes open for movement.

3. Satellites look like stars, only they are moving at a regular speed across the sky. How many satellites do you spot in 15 minutes? Were they all going the same direction? Or were they orbiting the planet on different paths? Did they travel at different speeds, or were they all evenly paced?

4. Experiment with the same activity at different times and compare your results.

active: Working.

astronauts: People who have been trained to fly aboard a spacecraft and work in space.

atmosphere: The mass of air surrounding Earth.

communications: A system for sending and receiving messages.

ground control: The Earth-based people and equipment that monitor and direct the operation of satellites and other spacecraft.

instruments: A tool or implement designed especially for precision work or a specific task.

Iraq: A landlocked country in the Middle East.

orbit: To travel around the sun or other object in space.

solar panels: Groups of solar cells; solar cells collect energy from the sun to make electricity.

spying: Secretly examining.

telescopes: Tools that makes faraway objects look larger and nearer; large telescopes can see deep into space.

INDEX

TO LEARN MORE

Learning more is as easy as 1, 2, 3.

1) Go to www.factsurfer.com

2) Enter "artificialsatellites" into the search box.

3) Click the "Surf" button to see a list of websites.

With factsurfer, finding more information is just a click away.